Do**Brilliantly**

KS3 English

The **best** approach to test preparation

- **Alan Coleby**
- **Kate Frost**
- **Series Editor: Jayne de Courcy**

Published by HarperCollins*Publishers* Ltd
77–85 Fulham Palace Road
London W6 8JB

www.**Collins**Education.com
On-line support for schools and colleges

First published 2001
Reprinted 2003
This new edition published 2004

10 9 8 7 6 5 4 3 2 1

ISBN 0 00 717097 1

Alan Coleby and Kate Frost assert the moral right to be identified as the authors of this work.

British Library Cataloguing in Publication Data
A catalogue record for this book is available from the British Library.

Edited by Mike Gould
Production by Katie Butler
Book design by Bob Vickers and Gecko Limited
Printed and bound by Printing Express, Hong Kong

Acknowledgements
The extracts in Paper 1 are reproduced from the following sources: *Tiger Woods* by Jack Clary (Tiger Books International, 1997); 'Through the Tunnel' by Doris Lessing, in *Short Stories of Our Time*, ed. Douglas R. Barnes (Thomas Nelson and Sons, 1984); *Biology for Life* by M. B. V. Roberts (Thomas Nelson and Sons, 1981).
Photographs
Lew Long/CORBIS (p.1); Tony Roberts/CORBIS (p.2); Roy Morsch/CORBIS (p.20).

Every effort has been made to contact the holders of copyright material, but if any have been inadvertently overlooked, the Publishers will be pleased to make the necessary arrangements at the first opportunity.

You might also like to visit:
www.**fire**and**water**.co.uk
The book lover's website

Contents

When is the Test?

You will sit your English National Test in May of Year 9. Your teacher will give you the exact dates.

What does the Test cover?

The English curriculum is divided into three Attainment Targets:

En 1 Speaking and Listening
En 2 Reading
En 3 Writing

The Test covers Reading and Writing. It also covers the Shakespeare play you have studied in Year 9. Your teacher will have chosen one play out of a list of three, and there are two scenes in your play which you will have studied in great detail.

How many papers are there?

There are **three** Test papers:

- Paper 1 tests your reading.
- Paper 2 and Paper 3 Section A test your writing.
- Paper 3 Section B tests you on two scenes of the Shakespeare play which you have studied.

Paper 1

There are three reading passages, with questions in a separate booklet.

The passages are likely to be:

- a passage of prose which is non-fiction (it does not tell a story); it could be a biography or an autobiography, a leaflet, a newspaper article, a diary, a travel book, a magazine article, a letter or an advertisement.

- a passage from a novel, short story or a poem.

- another passage from any non-fiction book such as a textbook or an instruction manual.

You are allowed 15 minutes to read the three passages and 1 hour to write your answers.

This paper carries 32 marks.

Paper 2

This paper has one writing task. You have 45 minutes to write your answer. The task is likely to be a story, or other form of narrative, where you can be as imaginative as you like, and you can control much of the form in which you write. This is called an 'open' task.

This paper carries 30 marks.

Paper 3

There are two sections to this paper, organised according to the play you have studied in class.

Section A

Here you are given another writing task, but shorter than that in Paper 2. You have 30 minutes to write your answer.

This is called a 'closed' or 'directed writing' task, which may be a letter, a speech, a report, a newspaper or magazine article, or a special account. The task will specify the form in which you must write.

The task is loosely linked to the theme, or subject, of the play you have studied, but you do not have to refer to the play in any way in order to answer it.

The task is worth 20 marks, which includes 4 marks for spelling.

Section B

This is a task about the Shakespeare play that you have studied. You have 45 minutes to answer it, including reading time. Three plays are set each year. Two scenes from each play are for detailed study, and your teacher will have told you which these are.

In 2004, these scenes are:

Henry V	Act 3 Scenes 1 and 2 (not Chorus)
	Act 4 Scene 7
Macbeth	Act 1 Scene 3
	Act 3 Scene 1
Twelfth Night	Act 2 Scene 3
	Act 4 Scene 2

There are passages from each scene printed on the Paper 3 Section B question paper, so you do not need to take a copy of the play into the Test.

This task is worth 18 marks.

ll students sit the same Test papers, and in English there is
ly one 'tier' resulting in the award of a level from 3 to 7.

v

How to do well in your Test

What is in this book

This book contains:

- complete Test Papers 1, 2 and 3
- the Shakespeare plays and scenes for 2004
- detailed answers and marking guidance

How to tackle Paper 1

You are given 15 minutes to read the three reading passages before you are allowed to write your answers. Make the best use of this time by reading all three passages thoroughly. Then, after noticing what the questions ask you about each passage, make notes on the inside cover of the answer booklet.

The questions sometimes advise you to refer to words and phrases from the passage to support the ideas you write about in your answers. This means that you should give quotations from the passage. Quotations are words and phrases or whole sentences copied from the passage. You must remember to put inverted commas in front of, and after, the words you copy.

There are two things to remember about using a quotation. First, do not make it too long, usually no longer than a sentence. Second, do not just pick out any phrase or sentence, but make it refer to the ideas that you have expressed in your own words in your answer.

Remember that when examiners mark answers to the questions, they do not mark writing style, spelling, punctuation, grammar, or paragraphing: they are concerned only with how well you have understood each passage and how relevant your answer is to the question.

Look hard at the mark allocation for each question as this will give you a guide as to how much to write. Spend longer on questions worth the most marks.

How to tackle Paper 2

You will be marked on 'Composition and effect' – how interesting what you write is, how appropriate the style you have chosen to write in is, and how well your writing engages the interest of your reader through your choice of vocabulary etc.

You will also be marked on how well you express yourself: 'Sentence structure and punctuation' and 'Text structure and organisation'.

Make sure that you use the planning sheet to plan your answer, paragraph by paragraph. This planning is not wasted time as it will allow you to write your story more quickly. It will also ensure that your story is carefully constructed with a powerful opening and ending.

Allow at least 5 minutes to check through your writing when you have finished. Don't worry if you want to change a word – for example, you may want to change an adjective for a more powerful one or add inverted commas around speech. Do any crossings-out as neatly as possible and you will not be penalised for this. In fact, you will be awarded higher marks if your editing of your writing has improved it – even if there are some crossings-out.

How to tackle Paper 3

Section A

The same advice applies to this as to Paper 2. However, with this task you need to check your spelling very carefully as 4 marks out of the possible 20 are allocated to spelling.

Remember that this is a directed task and that the form in which you need to write is specified in the question. You MUST use this form. If you do not, you will lose marks. Think hard about the conventions of the form required, whether it is a letter, a diary entry or an advertisement or newspaper article.

Make sure that you do not spend more than 30 minutes on this task. If you spend any longer, you will not have time to write a good answer to the section B task on your Shakespeare play.

Section B

Questions on the Shakespeare plays are most commonly of two types:

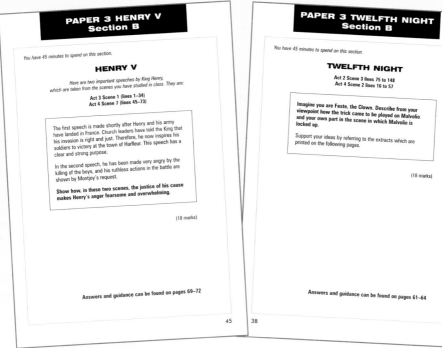

PAPER 3 HENRY V
Section B

You have 45 minutes to spend on this section.

HENRY V

Here are two important speeches by King Henry, which are taken from the scenes you have studied in class. They are:

Act 3 Scene 1 (lines 1–34)
Act 4 Scene 7 (lines 45–73)

The first speech is made shortly after Henry and his army have landed in France. Church leaders have told the King that his invasion is right and just. Therefore, he now inspires his soldiers to victory at the town of Harfleur. This speech has a clear and strong purpose.

In the second speech, he has been made very angry by the killing of the boys, and his ruthless actions in the battle are shown by Montjoy's request.

Show how, in these two scenes, the justice of his cause makes Henry's anger fearsome and overwhelming.

(18 marks)

Answers and guidance can be found on pages 69–72

45

PAPER 3 TWELFTH NIGHT
Section B

You have 45 minutes to spend on this section.

TWELFTH NIGHT

Act 2 Scene 3 lines 75 to 148
Act 4 Scene 2 lines 16 to 57

Imagine you are Feste, the Clown. Describe from your viewpoint how the trick came to be played on Malvolio and your own part in the scene in which Malvolio is locked up.

Support your ideas by referring to the extracts which are printed on the following pages.

(18 marks)

Answers and guidance can be found on pages 61–64

38

1 A 'critical discussion' question will ask you about aspects of plot, character, meaning or language in the scene.

2 An 'empathetic' question will ask you to imagine that you are one of the characters and to write as if you are that person.

The first of these types of question, 'critical discussion', is the most frequently set. Remember that in your answer to such a question you must include quotations. Do not make these quotations too long (two or three lines at the most), and make them refer clearly to the ideas you express in your own words.

With the second of these types of question, it is important to show that you know what all the other characters think, do and say, as well as concentrating on your particular character.

How to work out your marks and calculate your level

Paper 1

Add up the marks that you have achieved across all the questions on all three passages.

Paper 2

Use the marking grids on pages 23–25 to award yourself 'best-fit' marks for 'Sentence structure and punctuation', 'Text structure and organisation' and 'Composition and effect'.

Paper 3

Section A

Use the three marking grids on pages 50–52, 58–60 and 66–68 to award yourself 'best-fit' marks for your writing.

Section B

For this, the 'How well did you do?' section gives an extract from an answer at each level, along with a range of marks. First you need to decide which level your answer is at. Then you have to give yourself a mark from within the range given. You need to decide, for example, whether your answer is a good level 5, in which case you would award yourself the top mark possible, or whether it is a poor level 5, in which case you would award yourself the mark at the bottom of the range.

The first table below gives the marks and levels for each paper. The second table gives your level for the three papers together, based on your total mark.

Level	P1	P2	P3A	P3B
3	1–5	1–4	1–4	1–2
4	6–12	5–9	5–8	3–6
5	13–19	10–16	9–12	7–10
6	20–25	17–23	13–16	11–14
7	26–32	24–30	17–20	15–18

Level	Total
3	4–18
4	19–38
5	39–60
6	61–81
7	82–100

Energy for life

Paper 1: Reading

On the following pages you will find three reading texts:

1. An extract from the biography of the American golfer, Tiger Woods

2. The conclusion of a short story by Doris Lessing

3. *Getting Energy from Food*, an extract from a Science textbook

Remember

- You have 15 minutes to read these texts.

- During this time you must not write or open the Answer booklet.

- At the end of 15 minutes you will have 1 hour to answer the questions.

This extract is from the biography of the young American golfer, Tiger Woods.

Without a doubt, Tiger Woods is the result of his father's plan to raise a golf champion. Earl Woods was a good athlete, whose principal claim to athletic achievement was as a baseball catcher during a short time at Kansas State University. Woods was a career Army man who worked his way through the
5   ranks to the rank of lieutenant colonel when he fought in Vietnam. It was during his time in South East Asia that he met and married his second wife, Kultilda Punsawad. Six years later, their only son, Elrick, was born in Long Beach, California, on December 30, 1975.

    Earl Woods had big plans for his new son, and they mostly revolved around the
10   game of golf, to which Earl had been introduced a few years earlier. Earl has said that he was driven by the fact that as a black, he had long been denied access to the country-club world of golf. 'But I told myself that somehow my son would get a chance to play golf early in life.' So before Tiger was even one year old, his father would take him out to the garage and put him in his high chair or playpen, where
15   the boy would watch his father pound ball after ball into a practice net and putt ball after ball into a cup.

    His father has said that when Tiger was just ten months old, he took up a putter and gave a perfect display of the delicate art of putting a golf ball. When he was three, he won a pitch, putt and drive competition against ten- and eleven-year-olds.
20   But his father didn't limit his instruction to the sheer mechanics of golf. During his years as a Green Beret, he had learned a great deal about shaping a mind to cope with stress, and so he set out to mould his son's mind so that he could master the all-important skill of concentration. At age six, while Tiger was out in his family's garage hitting balls into the same net he had watched his father use, he

was also listening to subliminal messages on a tape recorder. His father had also   25
tacked messages of positive reinforcement to Tiger's desk in his room. Earl
Woods used a mixture of distractions that could cause a golfer's game to fall
apart. His father did everything, from making caustic remarks before Tiger was
set to tee off or sink a putt, to making noise at the top of his backswing. In Earl's
own words, he pulled 'every nasty, dirty, ungodly trick on him.' This went on until   30
his father was satisfied that he could endure anything on a golf course and not
crack.

While Earl handled the golf course and the playing schedule when his job
allowed, as well as juggling the family's financial resources to help maintain Tiger's
playing needs, his wife provided strength and stability at home. She not only   35
served as a taxi service to Tiger's midweek golf matches, but more importantly,
she also saw to it that he responded to all the demands of family life. She insisted
that he conduct himself properly, and particularly that he adhere to the
gentlemanly protocols of golf. At the same time, she taught him some of her own
toughness, driving home the point that when he was ahead in a match he should   40
not let up, but instead, try as hard as he could to overwhelm an opponent. Then,
when the match was won, he was to be a sportsman.

The 'tough love' that Earl used to shape his son's character was nothing more
than solid parenting. For example, in his very early years, Tiger was given a set of
shortened clubs and when he looked in the bag and didn't see a 1-iron, the   45
hardest club to hit, he asked to have one. He was told he was still too young to
generate enough clubhead speed to use it effectively; but a while later, he was out
on the driving range, using his father's 1-iron – which was almost as long as he
was tall – so effectively that there was little doubt he could handle it. His dad
promptly went out and bought him one.   50

In 1997, Tiger Woods took part in the U.S. Masters golf tournament. He
became the youngest ever to win the title as well as the first to win the first
major he ever played in as a professional. His twelve-stroke victory margin was
the largest ever at the Masters, and the largest in any major championship this
century.   55

When he sank his final putt to make par on the 18th, he spun around and
churned his arm up and down, his patented punctuation mark to signify that he
had achieved something special. A few moments later, he was in the embrace
of his parents, dissolving into tears as he hugged his father for nearly a half
minute. 'I think more than anything I was relieved it was over,' Tiger said later. 'I   60
think every time I hug my mom or pop after a tournament, it's over. I
accomplished my goal. And to share it with them is something special.'

When he talked by phone with President Bill Clinton a few moments later,
the First Golfer told him: 'The best shot I saw all week was the shot of you
hugging your dad.'   65

Conclusion of a short story by Doris Lessing

Jerry, a young English boy in South Africa, and a very good swimmer, longed to be
accepted by a group of native boys. These boys were such good swimmers that they could
dive to the sea bed and swim through a long tunnel, underneath a wide barrier rock,
before surfacing the other side. Jerry wanted to show that he was as good as they were,
by swimming through the tunnel.

But even after he had made the decision, or thought he had, he found himself sitting up
on the rock and looking down into the water, and he knew that now, at this moment,
when his nose had only just stopped bleeding, when his head was still sore and
throbbing – this was the moment when he would try. If he did not do it now, he never

5   would. He was trembling with fear that he would not go, and he was trembling with
horror at that long, long tunnel under the rock, under the sea. Even in the open sunlight
the barrier rock seemed very wide and very heavy; tons of rock pressed down on where
he would go. If he died there he would lie until one day – perhaps not before next year
– those big boys would swim into it and find it blocked.

10   He put on his goggles, fitted them tight, tested the vacuum. His hands were shaking.
Then he chose the biggest stone he could carry and slipped over the edge of the rock until
half of him was in the cool, enclosing water and half in the hot sun. He looked up once
at the empty sky, filled his lungs once, twice, and then sank fast to the bottom with the
stone. He let it go and began to count. He took the edges of the hole in his hands and

15   drew himself into it, wriggling his shoulders in sideways as he remembered he must,
kicking himself along with his feet.

Soon he was clear inside. He was in a small rock-bound hole filled with yellowish-
grey water. The water was pushing him up against the roof. The roof was sharp and
pained his back. He pulled himself along with his hands – fast, fast – and used his legs

20   as levers. His head knocked against something; a sharp pain dizzied him. Fifty, fifty-one,
fifty-two…. He was without light, and the water seemed to press upon him with the
weight of rock. Seventy-one, seventy-two…. There was no strain on his lungs. He felt
like an inflated balloon, his lungs were so light and easy, but his head was pulsing.

He was being continually pressed against the sharp roof, which felt slimy as well as

25   sharp. Again he thought of octopuses, and wondered if the tunnel might be filled with
weed that could tangle him. He gave himself a panicky, convulsive kick forward, ducked
his head, and swam. His feet and hands moved freely, as if in open water. The hole must
have widened out. He thought he must be swimming fast, and he was frightened of
banging his head if the tunnel narrowed.

30   A hundred, a hundred and one…. The water paled. Victory filled him. His lungs were
beginning to hurt. A few more strokes and he would be out. He was counting wildly;
he said a hundred and fifteen, and then, a long time later, a hundred and fifteen again.
The water was a clear jewel-green all around him. Then he saw, above his head, a crack
running up through the rock. Sunlight was falling through it, showing the clean dark rock

35   of the tunnel, a single mussel shell, and darkness ahead.

He was at the end of what he could do. He looked up at the crack as if it were filled
with air and not water, as if he could put his mouth to it to draw in air. A hundred and

fifteen, he heard himself say inside his head – but he had said that long ago. He must go on into the blackness ahead, or he would drown. His head was swelling, his lungs cracking. A hundred and fifteen, a hundred and fifteen pounded through his head, and he feebly clutched at rocks in the dark, pulling himself forward, leaving the brief space of sunlit water behind. He felt he was dying. He was no longer quite conscious. He struggled on in the darkness between lapses into unconsciousness. An immense, swelling pain filled his head, and then the darkness cracked with an explosion of green light. His hands, groping forward, met nothing, and his feet, kicking back, propelled him out into the open sea.

He drifted to the surface, his face turned up to the air. He was gasping like a fish. He felt he would sink now and drown; he could not swim the few feet back to the rock. Then he was clutching it and pulling himself up on to it. He lay face down, gasping. He could see nothing but red-veined, clotted dark. His eyes must have burst, he thought; they were full of blood. He tore off his goggles and a gout of blood went into the sea. His nose was bleeding, and the blood had filled the goggles.

He scooped up handfuls of water from the cool, salty sea, to splash on his face, and did not know whether it was blood or salt water he tasted. After a time, his heart quieted, his eyes cleared, and he sat up. He could see the local boys, diving and playing half a mile away. He did not want them. He wanted nothing but to get back home and lie down.

In a short while, Jerry swam to shore and climbed slowly up the path to the villa. He flung himself on his bed and slept, waking at the sound of feet on the path outside. His mother was coming back. He rushed to the bathroom, thinking she must not see his face with bloodstains, or tearstains, on it. He came out of the bathroom and met her as she walked into the villa, smiling, her eyes lighting up.

'Have a nice morning?' she asked, laying her hand on his warm brown shoulder a moment.

'Oh, yes, thank you,' he said.

'You look a bit pale.' And then, sharp and anxious, 'How did you bang your head?'

'Oh, just banged it,' he told her.

She looked at him closely. He was strained. His eyes were glazed-looking. She was worried. And then she said to herself: 'Oh, don't fuss! Nothing can happen. He can swim like a fish.'

They sat down to lunch together.

'Mummy,' he said, 'I can stay under water for two minutes – three minutes, at least.' It came bursting out of him.

'Can you, darling?' she said. 'Well, I shouldn't overdo it. I don't think you ought to swim any more today.'

She was ready for a battle of wills, but he gave in at once. It was no longer of the least importance to go to the bay.

'Getting Energy from Food', an extract from a science textbook

Does food really contain energy?

We need energy to move, grow, mend our tissues when they are damaged, and just to keep ourselves alive. We get energy from our food. The energy contained in food used to be expressed in kilocalories, but this term has been replaced by kilojoules (kj). 4.2 kj of energy are required to raise the temperature of 1 kg of water through 1°C.

The amount of energy in a particular food depends on the substances which it contains. The three main kinds of food are carbohydrate, fat and protein. If we estimate the amount of energy in each of these, we can compare their energy values. Here they are:

Carbohydrate	1 gram contains 17 kj
Fat	1 gram contains 39 kj
Protein	1 gram contains 18 kj

Table 1 tells us how much energy there is in some everyday foods.

Table 1

	Kj per gram		Kj per gram
Margarine	32.2	White bread	10.6
Butter	31.2	Chips	9.9
Peanuts	24.5	Roast chicken	7.7
Milk chocolate	24.2	Eggs	6.6
Cake	18.8	Boiled potatoes	3.3
White sugar	16.5	Milk	2.7
Pork sausages	15.5	Bottled beer	1.2
Cornflakes	15.3	Boiled cabbage	0.34
Rice	15.0		

Thus, margarine and butter contain a lot of energy because they consist almost entirely of fat. At the other extreme, cabbage contains very little energy because it consists of a high percentage of water.

How much energy do we need each day?

Imagine someone lying in bed doing nothing. Even in such an inactive state, energy is needed to breathe, make the heart beat, and drive all those countless chemical reactions which keep us alive. The rate at which these 'ticking over' processes take place is called the 'basal metabolic rate'.

How much energy is needed to maintain the basal metabolic rate? It is difficult to say, because it varies from one individual to another. Very roughly, the amount needed is 7,000 kj per day. This is about the same amount of energy that would be needed to boil enough water for 100 cups of tea. This figure applies to a person who is completely at rest. It doesn't even include the energy she needs to feed herself. Scientists have tried to work out how much energy an average person needs to get through the day with the minimum effort, i.e. to get up in the morning, eat and drink and do other essential tasks, but no more. The figure is about 9,200 kj per day. A person could get enough energy to satisfy this need by eating one large white loaf a day, though, of course, this would not be a balanced diet.

Few of us spend our days like that – most of us do something. Table 2 tells us roughly how much energy is needed each day by different people.

Table 2

	Kj per day
Child 1 year old	3,000
Child 5–7 years old	7,500
Girl 12–15 years old	9,500
Boy 12–15 years old	12,000
Office worker	11,000
Factory worker	12,500
Heavy manual worker	15,000
Pregnant woman	10,000

The amount depends upon the person's age, sex and occupation. A person who spends most of the time sitting down needs far less energy than a very active person.

What happens when we eat too much?

Suppose a person eats more food than is needed for producing enough energy. What happens to the food left over? Most of it is turned into fat and stored beneath the skin. The result is that body weight increases, and he or she runs the risk of becoming fat (or obese). Obesity is caused by a person's energy input being greater than the energy output.

The most 'fattening' foods are those which provide the most energy, such as bread and margarine, cake and sweets.

How can a person lose weight? The only way is by making his or her energy input less than the output. This can be done in two different ways:

1   By taking more exercise: this will increase the energy output.

2   By eating less energy-containing food: this will decrease the energy input.

75   The first method is not very effective. A person has to take a lot of exercise to make much difference to his or her weight. For example, a man trying to lose weight may play a game of tennis for half an hour. In doing so, he loses about 700 kj of energy. After the game, he feels thirsty and has a glass of beer. The result is that he puts back all the energy he has just lost.

80   The second method is very effective if carried out properly. A person on a well-planned, weight-reducing diet can lose about 1 kg per week. Such diets contain relatively little high-energy food and a lot of low-energy food.

    The best results can be obtained by combining both methods, i.e. by going on a weight-reducing diet and taking more exercise.

English test

Reading paper Energy for life answer booklet

First Name _____

Last Name _____

School _____

Write your answers in the spaces.

- The paper is 1 hour 15 minutes long.

- You have 15 minutes to read the Reading passages before answering the questions. During this time do not begin to write.

- You then have 1 hour to write your answers.

- There are 13 questions totalling 32 marks on this paper.

n

STAGE

ELS
–7

004

Answer the following questions.

Questions 1-4 are about Tiger Woods. (pages 2–3)

1 Underline the words from the following list which describe qualities that Tiger's parents taught him:

Concentration; selfishness; determination; craftiness; stability; recklessness; responsibility.

(1 mark)

2 Here is a list of events in Tiger's early life. Number them in the order in which they occur. The first one has been done for you.

1 Elrick Woods was born in Long Beach, California, in 1975.

His father tacked messages to Tiger's desk in his room.

He took up a putter and gave a perfect display of putting a golf ball.

He won a pitch, putt and drive competition against much older golfers.

He watched his father putt ball after ball into a cup.

He was out on the driving-range, using his father's 1-iron.

He asked for a 1-iron.

(1 mark)

3 What caused Tiger's father to be determined that his son would play golf well?

(3 marks)

4 The paragraph in which Tiger's father's tricks are described is linked with the one explaining his mother's role.
Write down the link sentence. Explain his mother's part in Tiger's upbringing.

(5 marks)

Questions 5-9 are about Jerry and his swimming.
(pages 4–5)

5   Before Jerry sank to the bottom of the sea, he felt a number of emotions. Underline
two of the following feelings that he had:

fear; jealousy; spite; horror; joy.   (1 mark)

6   Pick out and write down the short sentence in the second paragraph which most
strongly describes the state of Jerry's nerves.

--- (1 mark)

7   Why did Jerry carry a stone with him as he got into the water?

--- (2 marks)

8   In the fifth paragraph, there is the short sentence, 'Victory filled him' (line 30).
Here, the writer is using a metaphor: that is, the boy cannot literally be filled
with 'victory' because it is just an idea, but the writer is expressing it that way,
to strengthen the idea. Find two more phrases in the same paragraph where the
writer does this.

--- (2 marks)

9   There was a great tension and excitement in the writing as Jerry struggled to
swim through the tunnel and out into the open sea before he could breathe
again. In the paragraph beginning, 'He drifted to the surface' (line 47), describe
Jerry's feelings in your own words.
What does the reader feel at this point?

--- (4 marks)

Questions 10-13 are about the passage 'Getting energy from food.' (pages 6–8)

10 Words are often joined by a hyphen (we call them 'compounds') so that an idea can be expressed in a shorter, more effective way. These two compounds occur near the end of the passage. For each one, rewrite the same idea in your own words:

    'well-planned';   'weight-reducing'.

--- (2 marks)

11 Explain why a prisoner who is not allowed out of his cell does not necessarily put on weight.

--- (2 marks)

12 The author uses questions sparingly, but they occur three times at the beginning of paragraphs, at important points in the argument. Each time, there is no need to use a question. Why do you think the author does so?

--- (3 marks)

13 Do you think it is the author's purpose to persuade people to eat more low-energy food, and so reduce weight?

--- (5 marks)

elow you will find possible answers to the Reading Test questions, with the marks awarded for hose answers. Compare your answers with those that are given to see how close you came to hem and whether you would have achieved the same mark.

1   The words that should be underlined are:

Concentration; determination; stability; responsibility.

Total marks: 1 (All 4 correct)

Examiner's comment

This question allows you to show an understanding of the writer's use of language at word level, and to show an understanding of the passage by interpreting information at text level.

2   The correct order is:

1   **Elrick Woods was born in Long Beach, California, in 1975.**

5   **His father tacked messages to Tiger's desk in his room.**

3   **He took up a putter and gave a perfect display of putting a golf ball.**

4   **He won a pitch, putt and drive competition against much older golfers.**

2   **He watched his father putt ball after ball into a cup.**

7   **He was out on the driving range, using his father's 1-iron.**

6   **He asked for a 1-iron.**

Total marks: 1 (This order must be totally correct)

Examiner's comment

This question enables you to show understanding of the whole passage by selecting information from different parts of it.

3   **'Because he liked the game and he had big plans for his son.'**

There are 3 marks for this question, and this answer scores none because, although what it says is true, this is not the main or most important reason for Earl's wanting Tiger to play well. This answer also uses words from the passage, instead of the pupil using his own words. Therefore, there are no marks for this answer.

'Because Earl was keen on the game but he had long been denied access to the country-club world of golf because he was black.'

This scores 1 mark because although the important point about why Earl wanted Tiger to play well is understood, it is not clearly stated, and indeed does not mention Tiger at all. In addition, some of it is just copied from the passage, and so the marker does not really know whether the pupil understands the point. Although there are no marks specifically for the style, this answer is poorly expressed, as it is not written correctly in a sentence. Therefore, 1 mark.

'Earl Woods wanted his son to play golf well, because, as a black man, he had been kept out of the well-to-do world of golf clubs.'

This scores 2 marks because, although it is now correctly written in the pupil's own words, it does not mention that Earl himself played well, and it does not say what it was that he wanted his son to do. Therefore, 2 out of 3 marks.

'Because he was a black man, Earl Woods had been excluded from the comfortable, luxurious world of golf clubs, in spite of the fact that he played well. This is what made him determined that his son would play well enough to enter the golf-club world which had been denied him.'

This scores 3 out of 3. It is well expressed in correct sentences and mentions all the relevant aspects of the situation, including Earl Woods' motivation.

Total marks: 3

Examiner's overall comment

This question enables you to comment on the writer's purpose and viewpoint, as well as showing an understanding of the passage at sentence and text levels.

4   The link sentence is: **'While Earl handled the golf course and the playing schedule when his job allowed, as well as juggling the family's financial resources to help maintain Tiger's playing needs, his wife provided strength and stability at home.'**

There is 1 mark for the whole sentence. The whole sentence is the full answer because it balances the roles of both parents and is therefore the link.

'Tiger's mother was a taxi service to get him to his matches. She made him behave himself at matches and taught him some of her own toughness.'

This would score 1 out of 4 marks for this question. Three of the four roles his mother played are mentioned, but most of the phrases are copied from the text.

'Tiger's mother ran him everywhere he needed to go to golf matches, and made him take part in family life. She insisted on good conduct, and taught him how to be tough when he was ahead in a match.'

This scores 2 out of 4 marks. All the four roles that his mother fulfilled are covered, though in a superficial way, which probably shows only a surface understanding of the text.

'Tiger's mother had to provide transport to and from his golf matches, and also made him play his full role in family life. She was also keen on him behaving properly and like a gentleman on the golf course. However, she did not forget to teach him to have a tough attitude towards his opponent at golf.'

This scores 3 out of 4 marks. Each role played by his mother is described in the pupil's own words and the idea that his behaviour should be appropriate to different situations is introduced.

'Tiger's mother was obviously a strong and well-balanced person, for not only did she work hard for Tiger in the sense of providing transport for his golf matches, but she also dominated him by insisting that he played a full role in family life, for which he would have to work hard himself. Under her watchful eye, on the golf course he would have to behave properly like a gentleman. However, because of her toughness, she taught him to remain highly competitive towards his opponents until the match was over, when he should resume being a gentleman.'

This answer scores 4 marks out of 4. Each different aspect of her influence on Tiger is set in the context of her personality, and shows a thorough understanding of the passage as a whole.

The total mark for this question is therefore 1 + 4 = 5.

Examiner's overall comment

This question enables you to show an understanding of the writer's purpose and viewpoint, to interpret information, and to comment on the structure and organisation of the text.

5   **Fear. Horror.**   Total mark: 1 (Both must be correct)

Examiner's comment

This question allows you to show an understanding of the writer's use of language at word level.

---

6   **'His hands were shaking'** (1 mark)

The full sentence is required.   Total mark: 1

Examiner's comment

This question allows you to show an understanding of the writer's use of language at sentence level.

---

7   **So that he could sink** (1 mark) **more quickly** (1 mark) *or* **fast** (1 mark).   Total marks: 2

Examiner's comment

This question allows you to show an understanding of the writer's use of language at sentence level.

---

8   **'Sunlight was falling'** (1 mark)   **'a crack running up'** (1 mark)   Total marks: 2

Examiner's comment

This question allows you to show an understanding of the writer's use of language at metaphorical and sentence levels.

---

9   *Marks are awarded only for the* **feelings** *identified.*
It does not matter what else is said about Jerry or about the reader, and it does not matter how well the answer is expressed. It is only the descriptions of Jerry's and the reader's feelings that matter.

For Jerry: **weakness; tiredness; exhaustion; relief; happiness; a sense of achievement; fear** (**'His eyes must have burst'**); **desperation** (**'He tore off his goggles'**). Any one of these scores 1/2 mark to a maximum of 2.

For the reader: **relief; suspense; anxiety; continuing excitement; happiness; continuing tension; apprehension; uncertainty.** Any one of these scores 1/2 mark to a maximum of 2.

No one will think of all the words for the feelings, and other words may be thought of and credited with a mark if the examiner thinks they are acceptable. That is why there is a maximum of 2 for each person.

Total marks: 4
(round up to whole marks)

Examiner's comment

Here, you can show an understanding of the writer's use of language at text level and an ability to empathise with the leading character.

10 1 mark for an answer which shows an adequate understanding of the compound; 1 mark for a thorough understanding; none for a misunderstanding.

Examples:

Well-planned: **'a plan is needed'** (0 marks)
                    'good planning' or **'planned efficiently and in detail'** (1 mark)

Weight-reducing: **'putting on weight'** (0 marks)
                    'taking off weight' or **'weight is deliberately lost in this way'** (1 mark)

Total marks: 2

Examiner's comment

This question enables you to show an understanding of the author's use of language at word level.

---

11 *The basic idea will be that a prisoner will have a low energy output, but will not put on weight if he eats low-energy food. Marks will be awarded according to how thoroughly this is understood and the detail in which it is expressed.*

'A prisoner who does not leave his cell will not put on weight if he eats low-energy food.'

1 mark here because both sides of the problem are understood, though the first is only implied, and there is little detail in the answer.

'A prisoner who is allowed no exercise will not put on weight if he eats low-energy food such as milk, eggs and vegetables.'

2 marks here because of a thorough understanding of the question and its answer, using material from the passage, with sufficient detail.

Total marks: 2

Examiner's overall comment

This question allows you to show an understanding of the writer's purpose and viewpoint so well that you can apply it to another situation.

---

12 *This question is awarded marks according to how well the pupil has understood the use of questions to mark the stages at which the author moves on to the next problem concerning the energy-producing capacity of food.*

Examples:

'The questions make you think about food energy' (1 mark);
'The questions focus the person's mind on the problems of energy-producing food' (2 marks);
'The questions concentrate the reader on the next stage of thinking about energy-producing food' (3 marks);

Total marks: 3

Examiner's overall comment

This question enables you to identify the author's purpose by commenting on the structure and organisation of the whole text.

13   *1 mark is awarded for the expression of an opinion, whatever it is.*

Either: **Yes, it is the author's purpose to persuade people to eat low-energy food.**
Or: **No, it is not his purpose to persuade people to eat low-energy food.**
Or: **The passage is purely factual, presented in an impartial, neutral way.**

Most marks are awarded for the evidence given in support of the opinion.
Not many marks would be given for big slices of the passage just copied down.
The way the facts are used determines the quality of the answer.

'The author persuades you to eat less, because if you don't use up the food, you get fat.'

This scores one mark because the idea is crude and basic, but correct.

'The author persuades you to eat less energy by saying what energy common foods have and then how much a person uses, so if you eat more than you use, you get fat.'

This scores two marks because the general idea is understood, but it is short and poorly organised.

'It is his purpose to persuade people to eat more low-energy food because he gives a lot of information about how much energy is contained in some common foods and then some figures to show the energy used by different kinds of people. Then he tells us that what happens when we eat too much is that the extra food turns into fat, and so we should eat less energy-producing food.'

This scores three marks. It is a better balanced answer, and includes the whole argument, but there is no detail, and it is not well organised.

'I think the author's purpose is not to persuade people in any way, but to present the facts about the energy produced by food and about how much energy is needed for an average day by people, according to age, sex and occupation. He does say how excess energy causes obesity, and how fat can be reduced by diet or exercise, but the facts are just presented, and he does not say obesity is bad, or try to persuade the reader to eat low-energy foods.'

This scores four marks. All parts of the argument are sensibly presented, with some amount of detail.

Total marks: 1 + 4 = 5

Examiner's overall comment

This question enables you to identify the writer's purpose by selecting evidence for it from different parts of the passage.

Overall total: 32 mark

Where to find more help

If you have not scored full marks on all these questions, then you will find lots of guidance on how to tackle Reading Test questions in *Collins Total Revision KS3 English*.

English test

Paper 2: Writing

n

STAGE

VELS

–7

004

First Name _____

Last Name _____

School _____

- ■ Write your work on lined paper.

- ■ The paper is 45 minutes long, including 15 minutes' planning time.

- ■ There is one task which has 30 marks.

- ■ Plan your work on the planning page opposite the task.

- ■ Write your answer in the Writing paper answer booklet.

Game On!

Write the story of any physical activity in which you have taken part.

This could be anything, from a football, hockey, cricket or netball match, to skating or swimming, or a ride in a fairground or theme park, or just going for a walk.

Whatever you write about, include:

- thoughts and feelings you have before the event;
- a description of what you did;
- your feelings of satisfaction or pleasure which were produced by the activity.

Use this page to plan your work. (This page will not be marked.)

Thoughts and feelings before event

-
-
-
-
-

What you did

What happened

Any problems or difficulties

How it ended

Feelings

-
-
-
-
-

Reasons for feelings

-
-
-
-
-

You need to decide what level your story would probably be awarded if you had written it in your Test. To do this, you need to read through the statements in each table and tick **the one** that you feel best applies to your story. That is then the mark that you should award yourself. Get an adult or friend to help you.

The statements in each table are arranged according to the criteria that examiners apply when they are marking Paper 2. They are organised in a hierarchy. This means that **the last** criterion in each table has the highest expectations in terms of the quality of your writing. If you can confidently tick this one in each table, then this means that you can award yourself the highest mark – and you are achieving a high level.

To work out your overall mark for Paper 2, you need to add together the marks you award yourself for 'Sentence structure and punctuation', 'Text structure and organisation' and 'Composition and effect'.

To assess your own work, use the tables which follow and put in the final columns the marks which you think **best fit** the description given. Where there is a **range**, you will need to decide whether your writing fits at the bottom, middle or top of the range.

Sentence structure and punctuation	Mark awarded	Your mark
A1 This band is included to show you what just falls short of Level 4 writing. – Mostly simple sentences with verbs in the past tense saying what happened. – Some common adjectives used. – Capital letters and full stops used, with perhaps an occasional comma.	0	
A2 – Some common connectives used (e.g. *because*, *when*, *if*) – Some variety of sentence subjects (e.g. 'My favourite match...', 'The best feeling....') – Some adverbial phrases ('After this...') – Capital letters and full stops used mostly correctly, with some other use of punctuation, such as speech marks.	1–2	
A3 – Use of connectives helps produce a more precise account (e.g. 'Although I was feeling tired...') – Some different verb tenses used ('I had been feeling exhausted, but then I recovered.') – Adverbial phrases add focus ('...by concentrating hard...') – Capital letters and full stops used mostly correctly, with some other punctuation marks.	3–4	
A4 – Use of clauses helps to develop the account (e.g. 'The ride was so enjoyable that we wanted to carry on....'.) – Different verb tenses are used correctly, helped by the use of modals (e.g. 'I could have run faster, even though I was in the lead.') – Impersonal forms used to give variety (e.g. 'It was a great occasion'...) and information added by expanded noun phrases (e.g. ...'the excited beating of my heart') – Range of punctuation used accurately.	5–6	
A5 – Variety of sentence types used to add interest, mixing information with feelings and comments. – More complicated verb forms used – compound and complex sentences, including modals (e.g. 'If it had not been for the rain, the event might have lasted longer.') – Passive constructions help make the account sound more formal (e.g. 'In the blistering heat the athletes were treated for exhaustion.') – Wide range of punctuation gives clarity and sometimes effect, such as semi-colons to balance ideas in a sentence.	7	
A6 – Wide range of sentence structures used to control the account, using a mixture of short, simple sentences/complex/embedded sentences (e.g. 'Carla, because she was so fit, was an easy winner.') – Wide range of punctuation used to create effects.	8	

Text structure and organisation	Mark awarded	Your mark
B1	This band is included to show you what just falls short of Level 4 writing. – Simple overall structure of story, signalled perhaps by a title or opening remark about an activity. Paragraphs sometimes used. – Ideas mostly linked by events in the order in which they took place.	0	
B2	– Story has a clear structure with some use of paragraphs to say what happened, but with very little comment on feelings. – Paragraphs started by topic sentences (e.g. 'I got excited....') – Sections on thoughts and feelings may be awkward or obvious ('Then I thought that...')	1–2	
B3	– Paragraphs help structure of story by separating the account from comments. Some attempt to link paragraphs (e.g. 'Five minutes later....') – Within paragraphs, ideas developed by details (e.g. 'Eric was glad to be taking part because...')	3–4	
B4	– Across the whole story, paragraphs vary in length and sentence types, linked by connectives and connecting phrases (e.g. 'however', 'because of this'...) to form a complete piece. – Ideas within paragraphs are linked by relevant detail and description to build up to the ending.	5–6	
B5	– The whole story is shaped towards interesting storytelling, (e.g. the ending resolves ideas or events from other parts of the story and gives a thoughtful comment on them). – A range of techniques helps fluency within paragraphs, e.g. moving from the general to the specific (e.g. 'The spectators were hushed...' 'One voice suddenly cheered...')	7	
B6	– The whole story is shaped and controlled for the interest and entertainment of the reader. – Within paragraphs a range of techniques draws in the reader with e.g. concluding questions, personal observations and opinions economically and precisely made (e.g. 'What a time we had that day! Could life get any better than this?')	8	

Composition and effect		Mark awarded	Your mark
C1	This band is included to show you what just falls short of Level 4 writing. – There are some features of a story or account (narrative). – The first person narrative is mostly maintained. – The account is mostly events with perhaps some thoughts added on at the end.	0	
C2	The main features of a story, e.g. title, opening, conclusion are present. Suitable selection of Content. – The first person narrative is maintained. – There is some mention of thoughts before the event or feelings afterwards.	1–3	
C3	– The features of the story grab the reader's attention, e.g. in the build-up to the event at the beginning. – There is selection of some detail in describing the event. – The first person narrative allows personal comments in the opening and ending. – Personal, emotive comments are there to add interest.	4–6	
C4	– Use of storytelling techniques, e.g. direct speech, talking to the reader directly keep the reader's interest. – The narrative includes both thoughts and feelings. – The choice of narrative features gives impact to the events, e.g. metaphorical language (similes, metaphors, personification)	7–9	
C5	The story is planned to manipulate reader e.g. by deliberate sequencing of material (not necessarily in chronological order) to lead to the climax or ending – The narrative has a distinctive style e.g. to add humour – The overall style is suitable for effective storytelling.	10–12	
C6	– Skilled use of storytelling techniques shows originality and interests and entertains the reader. – The narrative viewpoint is effective and convincing. – A definite style is maintained to explore the incident and support the chosen viewpoint.	13–14	

How to improve your story

If you feel you need extra help on writing a story, then you will find it in *Total Revision KS3 English*, also published by Collins Educational.

English test

Paper 3: Shakespeare

STAGE

ELS

–7

004

The paper is **1 hour and 15 minutes** long.

You may choose to write about one of three Shakespeare plays.

- *Macbeth*
- *Twelfth Night*
- *Henry V*

Whichever Shakespeare play you choose, the paper has **two sections**:

Section A assesses your writing and has **20 marks**;
Section B assesses your reading and understanding of your chosen play and has **18 marks**

Turn to **page 28** for the *Macbeth* paper

Turn to **page 37** for the *Twelfth Night* paper

Turn to **page 44** for the *Henry V* paper

Remember you should spend no more than 30 minutes on this section.

In *Macbeth*, the witches predict the future; at fairgrounds, gypsy fortune tellers do the same thing, either by gazing into a crystal ball or by reading palms.

HOW MUCH SHOULD YOU BELIEVE?

Your best friend has consulted the fortune teller at the local visiting fair.
She/he heard nothing but doom and gloom about his/her future, including predictions of illness and death.

You need to give your friend some advice on how to cope with it all.

Write down what you say to your friend to make him/her feel better.

(20 marks, including 4 marks for spelling)

Answers and guidance can be found on pages 49–52

You have 45 minutes to spend on this section.

MACBETH

Act 1 Scene 3 lines 37 to 141
Act 3 Scene 1 lines 1 to 71

In these two scenes, show how Shakespeare makes his characters use language to deceive one another.

Support your ideas by referring to the extracts which are printed on the following pages.

(18 marks)

Answers and guidance can be found on pages 53–56

Reading extracts for
MACBETH

In this extract, Macbeth meets the witches for the first time.

Act 1 Scene 3 (lines 37 to 141)

Enter MACBETH *and* BANQUO

MACBETH   So foul and fair a day I have not seen.

BANQUO   How far is't call'd to Forres? What are these,
            So wither'd and so wild in their attire,
            That look not like th'inhabitants o' the earth,   40
            And yet are on't? Live you? or are you aught
            That man may question? You seem to understand me,
            By each at once her choppy finger laying
            Upon her skinny lips: you should be women,
            And yet your beards forbid me to interpret
            That you are so.

MACBETH   Speak, if you can: what are you?   45

1st WITCH   All hail, Macbeth! hail to thee, Thane of Glamis!

2nd WITCH   All hail, Macbeth! hail to thee, Thane of Cawdor!

3rd WITCH   All hail, Macbeth! that shalt be king hereafter.

BANQUO   Good sir, why do you start, and seem to fear
            Things that do sound so fair? I' the name of truth,   50
            Are ye fantastical, or that indeed
            Which outwardly ye show? My noble partner
            You greet with present grace and great prediction
            Of noble having and of royal hope,
            That he seems rapt withal: to me you speak not.   55
            If you can look into the seeds of time,
            And say which grain will grow and which will not,
            Speak then to me, who neither beg nor fear
            Your favours nor your hate.

1st WITCH	Hail!	60
2nd WITCH	Hail!	
3rd WITCH	Hail!	
1st WITCH	Lesser than Macbeth, and greater.	
2nd WITCH	Not so happy, yet much happier.	
3rd WITCH	Thou shalt get kings, though thou be none: So, all hail, Macbeth and Banquo!	65
1st WITCH	Banquo and Macbeth, all hail!	

MACBETH Stay, you imperfect speakers, tell me more:
By Sinel's death I know I am Thane of Glamis;
But how of Cawdor? the Thane of Cawdor lives,   70
A prosperous gentleman; and to be king
Stands not within the prospect of belief
No more than to be Cawdor. Say from whence
You owe this strange intelligence or why
Upon this blasted heath you stop our way   75
With such prophetic greeting? Speak, I charge you.

WITCHES *vanish*

BANQUO The earth hath bubbles, as the water has,
And these are of them. Whither are they vanish'd?

MACBETH Into the air, and what seem'd corporal,
Melted, as breath into the wind. Would they had stay'd!   80

BANQUO Were such things here as we do speak about?
Or have we eaten on the insane root
That takes the reason prisoner?

MACBETH Your children shall be kings.

BANQUO You shall be king.

MACBETH And Thane of Cawdor too; went it not so?   85

BANQUO To the self-same tune and words. Who's here?

31

Enter ROSS *and* ANGUS

ROSS   The king hath happily received, Macbeth,
The news of thy success; and when he reads
Thy personal venture in the rebels' fight,
His wonders and his praises do contend   90
Which should be thine or his. Silenc'd with that,
In viewing o'er the rest o' the self-same day,
He finds thee in the stout Norweyan ranks,
Nothing afeard of what thyself didst make,
Strange images of death. As thick as hail   95
Came post with post, and every one did bear
Thy praises in his kingdom's great defence,
And pour'd them down before him.

ANGUS   We are sent
To give thee from our royal master thanks;
Only to herald thee into his sight,   100
Not pay thee.

ROSS   And for an earnest of a greater honour,
He bade me, from him, call thee Thane of Cawdor:
In which addition, hail, most worthy thane!
For it is thine.

BANQUO   What! can the devil speak true?   105

MACBETH   The Thane of Cawdor lives: why do you dress me
In borrowed robes?

ANGUS   Who was the thane lives yet;
But under heavy judgment bears that life
Which he deserves to lose.
Whether he was combin'd with those of Norway,   110
Or did line the rebel with hidden help
And vantage, or that with both he labour'd
In his counry's wrack, I know not;
But treasons capital, confess'd and prov'd,
Have overthrown him.

| MACBETH | (*aside*)   Glamis, and Thane of Cawdor: | 115 |

MACBETH   (*aside*)   Glamis, and Thane of Cawdor: 115
The greatest is behind.
(*To* ROSS *and* ANGUS) Thanks for your pains.
(*To* BANQUO) Do you not hope your children shall be kings,
When those that gave the Thane of Cawdor to me
Promis'd no less to them?

BANQUO   That, trusted home,
Might yet enkindle you unto the crown,   120
Beside the Thane of Cawdor. But 'tis strange:
And oftentimes, to win us to our harm,
The instruments of darkness tell us truths,
Win us with honest trifles, to betray's
In deepest consequence.   125
Cousins, a word, I pray you.

MACBETH   (*aside*)   Two truths are told,
As happy prologues to the swelling act
Of the imperial theme. I thank you, gentlemen.
(*aside*) This supernatural soliciting
Cannot be ill, Cannot be good; if ill,   130
Why hath it given me earnest of success,
Commencing in a truth? I am Thane of Cawdor:
If good, why do I yield to that suggestion
Whose horrid image doth unfix my hair
And make my seated heart knock at my ribs,   135
Against the use of nature? Present fears
Are less than horrible imaginings;
My thought, whose murder yet is but fantastical,
Shakes so my single state of mind that function
Is smother'd in surmise, and nothing is   140
But what is not.

Reading extracts for
MACBETH

In this extract, we see the relationship between Macbeth and Banquo deteriorating.

Act 3 Scene 1 (lines 1 to 71)

Forres, A room in the palace. Enter BANQUO

BANQUO	Thou hast it now: King, Cawdor, Glamis, all,	
	As the weird women promis'd; and, I fear,	
	Thou playd'st most foully for't; yet it was said	
	It should not stand in thy posterity,	
	But that myself should be the root and father	5
	Of many kings. If there come truth from them, –	
	As upon thee, Macbeth, their speeches shine –,	
	Why, by the verities on thee made good,	
	May they not be my oracles as well,	
	And set me up in hope? But, hush! no more.	10

Sennet sounded. Enter MACBETH, *as king;* LADY MACBETH, *as queen;* LENNOX, ROSS, LORDS, LADIES *and* ATTENDANTS

MACBETH	Here's our chief guest.	
LADY MACBETH	If he had been forgotten	
	It had been as a gap in our great feast,	
	And all-thing unbecoming.	
MACBETH	To-night we hold a solemn supper, sir,	
	And I'll request your presence.	
BANQUO	Let your highness	15
	Command upon me; to the which my duties	
	Are with a most indissoluble tie	
	For ever knit.	
MACBETH	Ride you this afternoon?	
BANQUO	Ay, my good lord.	20

MACBETH	We should have else desir'd your good advice – Which still hath been both grave and prosperous – In this day's council; but we'll take to-morrow. Is't far you ride?	
BANQUO	As far, my lord, as will fill up the time 'Twixt this and supper; go not my horse the better, I must become a borrower of the night For a dark hour or twain.	25
MACBETH	Fail not our feast.	
BANQUO	My lord, I will not.	30
MACBETH	We hear our bloody cousins are bestow'd In England and in Ireland, not confessing Their cruel parricide, filling their hearers With strange invention; but of that to-morrow, When therewithal we shall have cause of state Craving us jointly. Hie you to horse; adieu Till you return at night. Goes Fleance with you?	35
BANQUO	Ay, my good lord: our time does call upon's.	
MACBETH	I wish your horses swift and sure of foot; And so I do commend you to their backs. Farewell.	40

Exit BANQUO

	Let every man be master of his time Till seven at night; to make society The sweeter welcome, we will keep ourself Till supper-time alone; while then, God be with you!	45

Exeunt all but MACBETH *and an* ATTENDANT

	Sirrah, a word with you. Attend those men Our pleasure?	
ATTENDANT	They are, my lord, without the palace gate.	

MACBETH   Bring them before us.

Exit ATTENDANT

                To be thus is nothing;   50
But to be safely thus. Our fears in Banquo
Stick deep, and in his royalty of nature
Reigns that which would be fear'd: 'tis much he dares,
And, to that dauntless temper of his mind,
He hath a wisdom that doth guide his valour
To act in safety. There is none but he   55
Whose being I do fear; and under him
My genius is rebuk'd, as it is said
Mark Antony's was by Caesar. He chid the sisters
When first they put the name of king upon me,
And bade them speak to him; then, prophet-like,   60
They hail'd him father to a line of kings.
Upon my head they plac'd a fruitless crown,
And put a barren sceptre in my gripe,
Thence to be wrench'd with an unlineal hand,
No son of mine succeeding. If't be so,   65
For Banquo's issue have I fil'd my mind;
For them the gracious Duncan have I murder'd;
Put rancours in the vessel of my peace
Only for them; and mine eternal jewel
Given to the common enemy of man,   70
To make them kings, the seed of Banquo kings!

Remember you should spend no more than 30 minutes on this section.

In *Twelfth Night*, dressing-up is central to the plot.

DRESS UP OR LET US DOWN!

The last time your school had a 'non-uniform day' in order to raise money for charity, the response was poor.
You are a member of the school's charity fund-raising committee.

Write your speech for a school assembly, persuading the students in your school to support non-uniform day and contribute to a worthy cause.

(20 marks, including 4 marks for spelling)

Answers and guidance can be found on pages 57–60

You have 45 minutes to spend on this section.

TWELFTH NIGHT

Act 2 Scene 3 lines 75 to 148
Act 4 Scene 2 lines 16 to 57

Imagine you are Feste, the Clown. Describe from your viewpoint how the trick came to be played on Malvolio and your own part in the scene in which Malvolio is locked up.

Support your ideas by referring to the extracts which are printed on the following pages.

(18 marks)

Answers and guidance can be found on pages 61–64

Reading extracts for
TWELFTH NIGHT

In this extract, the drunken Sir Toby and Sir Andrew are told by Malvolio to improve their behaviour or leave Olivia's house, but Maria has a plan.

Act 2 Scene 3

Enter MALVOLIO

MALVOLIO	My masters, are you mad? Or what are you? Have you no wit, manners, nor honesty but to gabble like tinkers at this time of night? Do ye make an alehouse of my lady's house, that ye squeak out your coziers' catches without any mitigation or remorse of voice? Is there no respect of place, persons, nor time in you?	75
SIR TOBY	We did keep time, sir, in our catches. Sneck up!	80
MALVOLIO	Sir Toby, I must be round with you. My lady bade me tell you that, though she harbours you as her kinsman, she's nothing allied to your disorders. If you can separate yourself and your misdemeanors, you are welcome to the house; if not, and it would please you to take leave of her, she is very willing to bid you farewell.	85
SIR TOBY	[*Sings*] Farewell, dear heart, since I must needs be gone.	
MARIA	Nay, good Sir Toby.	
FESTE	[*Sings*] His eyes do show his days are almost done.	
MALVOLIO	Is't even so?	
SIR TOBY	[*Sings*] But I will never die.	90
FESTE	[*Sings*] Sir Toby, there you lie.	
MALVOLIO	This is much credit to you.	
SIR TOBY	[*Sings*] Shall I bid him go?	
FESTE	[*Sings*] What and if you do?	

SIR TOBY	[*Sings*] Shall I bid him go, and spare not?	95
FESTE	[*Sings*] O! no, no, no, no, you dare not.	
SIR TOBY	Out o' time, sir? Ye lie! Art any more than a steward? Dost thou think because thou art virtuous, there shall be no more cakes and ale?	
FESTE	Yes, by Saint Anne, and ginger shall be hot i'the mouth, too.	100
	[*Exit*]	
SIR TOBY	Th'art i'the right. Go, sir, rub your chain with crumbs. A stoup of wine, Maria!	
MALVOLIO	Mistress Mary, if you prized my lady's favour at anything more than contempt, you would not give means for this uncivil rule; she shall know of it, by this hand.	105
	Exit	
MARIA	Go shake your ears.	
SIR ANDREW	'Twere as good a deed as to drink when a man's a-hungry, to challenge him the field, and then to break promise with him, and make a fool of him.	
SIR TOBY	Do't, knight: I'll write thee a challenge; or I'll deliver thy indignation to him by word of mouth.	110
MARIA	Sweet Sir Toby, be patient for tonight. Since the youth of the count's was today with my lady, she is much out of quiet. For Monsieur Malvolio, let me alone with him. If I do not gull him into an ayword, and make him a common recreation, do not think I have wit enough to lie straight in my bed. I know I can do it.	115
SIR TOBY	Possess us, possess us, tell us something of him.	
MARIA	Marry, sir, sometimes he is a kind of puritan.	
SIR ANDREW	O if I thought that, I'd beat him like a dog!	120

SIR TOBY   What, for being a puritan? Thy exquisite reason, dear knight?

SIR ANDREW   I have no exquisite reason for't, but I have reason good
enough.

MARIA   The devil a puritan that he is, or anything constantly but a
time-pleaser; an affectioned ass, that cons state without book and   125
utters it by great swarths. The best persuaded of himself: so
crammed (as he thinks) with excellencies, that it is his grounds of
faith that all who look on him love him; and on that vice in him
will my revenge find notable cause to work.

SIR TOBY   What wilt thou do?   130

MARIA   I will drop in his way some obscure epistles of love; wherein
by the colour of his beard, the shape of his leg, the manner of his
gait, the expressure of his eye, forehead, and complexion, he shall
find himself most feelingly personated. I can write very like my lady
your niece; on a forgotten matter we can hardly make distinction   135
of our hands.

SIR TOBY   Excellent, I smell a device.

SIR ANDREW   I have't in my nose too.

SIR TOBY   He shall think, by the letters that thou wilt drop that they
come from my niece, and that she is in love with him.   140

MARIA   My purpose is, indeed, a horse of that colour.

SIR ANDREW   And your horse now would make him an ass.

MARIA   Ass, I doubt not.

SIR ANDREW   O 'twill be admirable!

MARIA   Sport royal, I warrant you: I know my physic will work with   145
him. I will plant you two, and let the fool make a third, where he
shall find the letter. Observe his construction of it. For this night,
to bed, and dream on the event. Farewell.

In this scene, Malvolio has been locked up for his strange behaviour but Sir Toby and the others continue to torment him. Feste dresses up as a priest and disguises his voice when he visits Malvolio in the dark chamber.

Act 4 Scene 2

FESTE   What ho, I say! Peace in this prison!

SIR TOBY   The knave counterfeits well; a good knave.

MALVOLIO   [*Within*] Who calls there?

FESTE   Sir Topas the curate, who comes to visit Malvolio the lunatic.

MALVOLIO   Sir Topas, Sir Topas, good Sir Topas, go to my lady.   20

FESTE   Out, hyperbolical fiend! How vexest thou this man! Talk'st thou nothing but of ladies?

SIR TOBY   Well said, Master Parson.

MALVOLIO   [*Within*] Sir Topas, never was man thus wronged. Good Sir Topas, do not think I am mad.They have laid me here in hideous darkness.   25

FESTE   Fie, thou dishonest Satan! I call thee by the most modest terms, for I am one of those gentle ones that will use the devil himself with courtesy. Sayst thou that the house is dark?

MALVOLIO   As hell, Sir Topas.

FESTE   Why, it hath bay-windows transparent as barricadoes, and the   30
clerestories toward the south-north are as lustrous as ebony; and yet complain'st thou of obstruction?

MALVOLIO   I am not mad, Sir Topas. I say to you, this house is dark.

FESTE   Madman, thou errest. I say there is no darkness but ignorance, in which thou art more puzzled than the Egyptians in their fog.   35

MALVOLIO   I say this house is as dark as ignorance, though ignorance
were as dark as hell; and I say there was never man thus abused.
I am no more mad than you are. Make the trial of it in any constant
question.

FESTE   What is the opinion of Pythagoras concerning wildfowl?   40

MALVOLIO   That the soul of our grandam might haply inhabit a bird.

FESTE   What think'st thou of his opinion?

MALVOLIO   I think nobly of the soul, and no way approve his opinion.

FESTE   Fare thee well. Remain thou still in darkness. Thou shalt hold
th'opinion of Pythagoras ere I will allow of thy wits, and fear to   45
kill a woodcock, lest thou dispossess the soul of thy grandam. Fare
thee well.

MALVOLIO   Sir Topas! Sir Topas!

SIR TOBY   My most exquisite Sir Topas!

FESTE   Nay, I am for all waters.   50

MARIA   Thou mightst have done this without thy beard and gown; he
sees thee not.

SIR TOBY   To him in thine own voice, and bring me word how thou
find'st him. I would we were well rid of this knavery. If he may
be conveniently delivered, I would he were, for I am now so far   55
in offence with my niece that I cannot pursue with any safety this
sport to the upshot. [*To* MARIA] Come by and by to my chamber.

Exit [*with* MARIA]

Remember you should spend no more than 30 minutes on this section.

One of the main aspects of 'Henry V' is the strength of Henry's character. As he says before attacking Harfleur, in normally peaceful times a man should be modest, patient and considerate, but when there is just cause to be stirred to action, he should be strong and relentless.

I WAS REALLY ANGRY!

Remember or imagine a time in your life when you suddenly felt that you could no longer be patient about a situation or about something that had happened. You became very angry. This might have been something in your family life, something at school or something involving your relationship with friends. It might have been something not affecting you that you saw and could not keep quiet about.

In a letter to a friend, write an account of what happened and why you felt angry.
There is no need to set out the letter in any formal way.

(20 marks, including 4 marks for spelling)

Answers and guidance can be found on pages 65–68

You have 45 minutes to spend on this section.

HENRY V

Here are two important speeches by King Henry,
which are taken from the scenes you have studied in class. They are:

Act 3 Scene 1 (lines 1–34)
Act 4 Scene 7 (lines 45–73)

The first speech is made shortly after Henry and his army have landed in France. Church leaders have told the King that his invasion is right and just. Therefore, he now inspires his soldiers to victory at the town of Harfleur. This speech has a clear and strong purpose.

In the second speech, he has been made very angry by the killing of the boys, and his ruthless actions in the battle are shown by Montjoy's request.

Show how, in these two scenes, the justice of his cause makes Henry's anger fearsome and overwhelming.

(18 marks)

Answers and guidance can be found on pages 69–72

Reading extracts for
HENRY V

In this extract, Henry is addressing his soldiers, inspiring them in their forthcoming battle against the citizens of Harfleur. There is an overwhelming sense of righteous anger.

Act 3 Scene 1 (lines 1–34)

France   Outside the walls of Harfleur

Enter the KING, BEDFORD *and* GLOUCESTER

Alarm. Enter soldiers with scaling ladders at Harfleur

KING HENRY   Once more unto the breach, dear friends, once more,
Or close the wall up with our English dead!
In peace there's nothing so becomes a man
As modest stillness and humility.
But when the blast of war blows in our ears,   5
Then imitate the action of the tiger:
Stiffen the sinews, conjure up the blood,
Disguise fair nature with hard-favoured rage.
Then lend the eye a terrible aspect,
Let it pry through the portage of the head   10
Like the brass cannon. Let the brow o'erwhelm it
As fearfully as doth a gallèd rock
O'erhang and jutty his confounded base,
Swill'd with the wild and wasteful ocean.
Now set the teeth and stretch the nostril wide,   15
Hold hard the breath, and bend up every spirit
To his full height. On, on, you noble English,
Whose blood is fet from fathers of war-proof,
Fathers that like so many Alexanders
Have in these parts from morn till even fought,   20
And sheathed their swords for lack of argument.
Dishonour not your mothers. Now attest
That those whom you called fathers did beget you.
Be copy now to men of grosser blood,

And teach them how to war.

                           And you, good yeomen,   25

Whose limbs were made in England, show us here

The mettle of your pasture. Let us swear

That you are worth your breeding, which I doubt not,

For there is none of you so mean and base

That hath not noble lustre in your eyes.   30

I see you stand like greyhounds in the slips,

Straining upon the start. The game's afoot.

Follow your spirit, and upon this charge

Cry 'God for Harry, England, and Saint George!'

Alarm, and chambers go off [*Exeunt*]

In this extract, the Battle of Agincourt is over, and Henry has won, but he is extremely angry because French soldiers, fleeing from the battle, have killed the defenceless young boys left in the English tents.

Act 4 Scene 7 (lines 45 – 73)

KING HENRY	I was not angry since I came to France	45
	Until this instant. Take a trumpet, herald.	
	Ride thou unto the horsemen on yon hill.	
	If they will fight with us, bid them come down,	
	Or void the field. They do offend our sight.	
	If they'll do neither, we will come to them,	50
	And make them skirr away as swift as stones	
	Enforcèd from the old Assyrian slings.	
	Besides, we'll cut the throats of those we have,	
	And not a man of them that we shall take	
	Shall taste our mercy. Go and tell them so.	55

[Exit English Herald]

Enter MONTJOY

EXETER   Here comes the herald of the French, my liege.

GLOUCESTER   His eyes are humbler than they used to be.

KING HENRY   How now, what means this, herald? Know'st thou not
That I have fined these bones of mine for ransom?
Com'st thou again for ransom?

MONTJOY	No, great king.	60
	I come to thee for charitable license,	
	That we may wander o'er this bloody field	
	To book our dead, and then to bury them,	
	To sort our nobles from our common men;	
	For many of our princes – woe the while –	65
	Lie drowned and soaked in mercenary blood;–	
	So do our vulgar drench their peasant limbs	
	In blood of princes, while the wounded steeds	
	Fret fetlock deep in gore, and with wild rage	
	Yerk out their armèd heels at their dead masters,	70
	Killing them twice. Oh, give us leave, great king,	
	To view the field in safety, and dispose	
	Of their dead bodies.	

ANSWERS AND GUIDANCE
Paper 3: Shakespeare
Sections A and B

MACBETH
Section A

The Test markers will assess your writing under the headings of:

'Composition and effect'
and
'Sentence structure, punctuation and text organisation'.

'Composition and effect' means the overall effect of your writing – the views you express, and the variety and stylistic features you use to get those views across to the reader, in this case, the Test marker.

'Sentence structure, punctuation and text organisation' means exactly what it says, and refers to the way you express yourself in terms of the sentences you use (for example, is what you say made clear by your choice of sentence structure?), the punctuation you select to organize those sentences – and the order and sequence of ideas *within* sentences and paragraphs.

There is also a further set of marks for spelling.

To assess your own writing, use the tables on the pages that follow and put in the final column the marks for your article which you think best fit the description given.

Composition and effect	Mark awarded	Your mark
You show some awareness of the task and who the advice is for, though remarks might not be backed up by reasons. A simple viewpoint is given, e.g. the idea that fortune-telling is rubbish but with no supporting evidence. You show awareness of a suitable style for advice (e.g. first person to express opinion) though this might lapse.	0	
You attempt to get the reader's interest by using a suitable tone ('It is terrible what she said to you…'). You keep up a consistent view, with some evidence to support your attitude to fortune tellers. Some suitable features of style help with giving opinions ('I don't know how I would have felt…').	1, 2, 3	
You use a consistent tone to keep the reader's attention e.g. helpful and friendly or consoling. You give a clear point of view e.g. by trying to put events in perspective ('You know, she was only a fairground gypsy…') Suitable features of style add interest, e.g. sharing a joke ('Don't you think her nose looked like a beak?')	4, 5, 6	
You keep the reader's interest by varying the approach, e.g. moving from discussing what was predicted to giving opinions and comments on the character of the fortune-teller. You develop a clear point of view e.g. by distinguishing between personal and others' views ('Some people would just laugh…I think that…'). You use different features of style to invite a response, e.g. to sum up, to ask questions ('What are we going to do about it?')	7, 8, 9	
You fulfil the purpose of the task by provoking a response in the reader, e.g. by making the reader want to give different advice. The tone adopted allows different views about fortune-telling to be addressed. Individual style is used to convey e.g. humour, sarcasm. ('She obviously couldn't foretell the winning lottery numbers or she wouldn't be working in a scruffy fairground!').	10	

Sentence structure, punctuation and text organisation	Mark awarded	Your mark
You use simple connectives (*and, but, so*) to link parts of sentences. You write mostly in the first person ('I') and use the present tense to give some opinions about fortune tellers or gypsies. You use simple adjectives to provide some basic details ('scary things', 'bad feelings'). You use capital letters and full stops in places.	0	
Your sentences are mostly correct with a little variety, e.g. connectives to explain ideas (e.g. 'When you were in the gypsy's caravan...') or different subjects of sentences to make things clearer ('Your hand was probably shaking....'; 'We were tired then....'). You use different verb types to help to explain ('When she was frowning, I thought that...'). Each section or paragraph is about a different part of what happened. Most capital letters and full stops are used correctly, with some other punctuation.	1, 2	
Some different sentence types help to give your opinions on the events ('If she hadn't surprised us so much, I might have...'). You use extra adjectives to give detail and attitudes ('an ugly, evil woman'). The main ideas in each section are supported by reasons. Nearly all sentences are correctly punctuated, with some punctuation within sentences.	3, 4	
You use different sentence lengths and types to add variety, e.g. subordinate clauses to support opinions ('Although fortune tellers are intriguing, they can also be disturbing...') You start sentences differently to emphasise points ('Despite frightening you out of your wits, she...'). Ideas are linked within paragraphs by the use of such things as lists leading to a climax ('After telling you...then she... finally...'), connecting phrases ('As soon as...'), and contrasts ('On the one hand...but you might say...'). You use punctuation reliably and clearly to mark the structure of your sentences.	5	
Your range of sentence types makes interesting reading. The variety of sentence types, lengths and verb forms develops your opinions and comments. Your advice is clear, logical and reassuring because of the arrangement of ideas within sections. You use a range of punctuation to make meaning clear and add to effects.	6	

Spelling	Mark awarded	Your mark
You have kept your words simple so that you can spell most of them, but you need to take care with words that sound the same, e.g. *there/their*; *were/ where*; *practice/practise*.	1	
You have tried to use bigger words, and have spelt the simple and common words correctly, but still need to be careful with words which sound the same, e.g. *weather/whether*; *affect/effect*.	2	
You can spell complex common and regular words correctly, but you may have problems with endings, e.g. *reducible/reducable*; *fulfil/fulfill*; *dependent/ dependant*. Combinations of vowels may also give you trouble, e.g. *receive/ recieve*; *brief/breif*; *weird/wierd*.	3	
You have tried to think of a wide range of vocabulary, so that you have used irregular and complicated words as well as common ones, and you have spelt most of them right. Your spelling is almost perfect apart from the occasional error.	4	

Total marks possible for Paper 3 Section A: 2

MACBETH
Section B

order to work out what level you would be awarded for the answer you have written, do the lowing:

Read the assessment guidance given **for each level.** (ie **Level 4**)

Then read carefully the **Typical remarks** section. This provides examples of the sorts of comments and points that will have been made by a student working at this level. Of course, you will not have written exactly the same remarks, but you should be able to tell if the **quality** of your writing is similar.

Now see if you can match *your* answer to a level. If you are unsure, ask someone you can trust – a relative or a friend – to help you.

Once you have decided what level your answer would probably be given, look at the column headed '**How to improve your level**'. This suggests what you need to do to improve your answer so that you can do better next time, and achieve a higher level.

How well did you do?

Level 4   *3-6 marks*

In a level 4 answer, there will be a little explanation showing some awareness of the more obvious ways the characters' speeches hide the truth, though there will be little detail. There will be some comment on the language used, with some reference to text.

Typical remarks in a level 4 answer:

n the first extract, the witches lead Macbeth on y telling him he will be king, but they don't tell im how it will happen. In the second extract, Macbeth and Banquo both pretend they are riends but we can see they don't really trust each ther, 'thou play'dst most foully for't'.

How to improve your level

1 Try to explain what each character is hoping to achieve by not being completely honest.

2 Use more quotations from the scenes to support what you say.

3 Comment on the quotations.

How well did you do?

Level 5 *7–10 marks*

A level 5 answer will show you understand the different ways Macbeth and the other characters speak to one another, though comments may not be developed. There will be awareness of the language through the use of textual quotations from both extracts.

Typical remarks in a level 5 answer:

During Act 1 Scene 3, the witches appear out of nowhere and surprise Macbeth. They speak directly to him, by name, 'All hail, Macbeth..', and they repeat one another's words. Banquo asks them to speak to him and again they take turns and speak in the same patterns. Their speeches are like riddles, 'Lesser than Macbeth and greater'.

In Act 3 Scene 1, we know from what they say when they are not together that Macbeth and Banquo are deadly enemies. At the beginning of the scene Banquo says, 'I fear, Thou play'dst most foully for't', which shows he no longer trusts him. They then have a friendly conversation about Banquo going out riding, but really Macbeth is just finding out his movements so that he can have him murdered. Macbeth is planning to have some ruffians carry out the deed so that he doesn't have to do it himself and it will be during the feast, so he will have an alibi.

How to improve your level

1 Give more details about the witches' predictions and more quotations from the scene. You might mention that Macbeth talks to himself, in soliloquies, quite a lot in this scene, so that the audience knows what he is thinking and can see that he does not always let his friends know what he really feels.

2 Describe the conversation about Banquo's ride in more detail, showing how Macbeth gets questions into the conversation to give him the information he needs.

3 You might compare how uncertain Macbeth is in the first extract with his absolutely calculating and decisive speeches in the second extract.

Level 6 *11–14 marks*

A level 6 answer will contain some discussion of how the witches speak in formal patterns to Macbeth and Banquo and how the audience will see the differences between the way Macbeth speaks in the two extracts.

Typical remarks in a level 6 answer:

In Act 1 Scene 3 the witches talk to Macbeth in a very formal way; they hail him, 'Thane of Glamis', 'Thane of Cawdor' and 'king hereafter', which is very shocking to Macbeth, as he only knows that he is Thane of Glamis at first, and later in the scene when he is given the second title, he is astounded. It makes him think about being king, and in a soliloquy to the audience he shows that he has already thought about it, saying: 'My thought, whose murder yet is but fantastical', but all the time he pretends to be a loyal subject to Duncan.

In the second extract we see that Banquo, too, does not always say what he means. When he is alone, he tells the audience of his suspicions, but when conversing with Macbeth, his language is flattering and apparently loyal. He says: 'my good lord', and 'my duties/ Are with a most indissoluble tie/ For ever knit'.

How to improve your level

1 Keep looking back at the wording of the task to make sure you have the right focus: here you are being asked about the characters in the extracts who don't say what they mean, indeed deliberately mislead the others, so try to mention all the ones which are relevant.

2 Remember this question focuses on language, so select quotations which will add to your comments on the characters and perhaps explain them further.

3 Try to put this task in the context of the whole play, as this will show that you really have understood it.

How well did you do?

Level 7   *15–18 marks*

A level 7 answer will focus clearly on language used to deceive and well-chosen quotations will support comments in your overall argument. It will analyse the way in which language is used to give the audience both information about the plot and insight into the characters.

Typical remarks in a level 7 answer:

A Shakespearean audience would be very familiar with the concept of witches and would know them to hold evil intent. When the sisters greet Macbeth formally, the first instinct of the two soldiers is not to take their words seriously, but the scene takes on a more sinister aspect when Ross and Angus confirm that Macbeth is indeed Thane of Cawdor, 'What! can the devil speak true?' says Banquo, and Macbeth lapses into reveries of what might be, in the form of asides to the audience which are at odds with what he says to his companions.

In the second extract there are many examples of characters using language to manipulate the situation: Banquo suspects Macbeth but is extremely polite to him, fearing what might happen; Macbeth is overly interested in Banquo's activities that afternoon, his good humour belying the fatal consequences for Banquo; the latter shows his uneasiness with the situation by giving very brief anwers to Macbeth's questions.

Where to find more help

Collins Total Revision KS3 English contains several chapters on how to answer questions on Shakespeare plays effectively.

TWELFTH NIGHT
Section A

The Test markers will assess your writing under the headings of:

- 'Composition and effect'

and

- 'Sentence structure, punctuation and text organisation'.

'Composition and effect' means the overall effect of your writing – the views you express, and the variety and stylistic features you use to get those views across to the reader, in this case, the Test marker.

'Sentence structure, punctuation and text organisation' means exactly what it says, and refers to the way you express yourself in terms of the sentences you use (for example, is what you say made clear by your choice of sentence structure?), the punctuation you select to organize those sentences – and the order and sequence of ideas *within* sentences and paragraphs.

There is also a further set of marks for spelling.

To assess your own writing, use the tables on the pages that follow and put in the final column the marks for your article which you think best fit the description given.

Composition and effect	Mark awarded	Your mark
You show some awareness of the task and who the speech is for, though remarks might not be backed up by reasons. A simple viewpoint is given, e.g. idea that fund-raising is good but with no supporting evidence. You show awareness of a suitable style for speech (e.g. second person to address audience) though this might lapse.	0	
You attempt to get the listener's interest by using a suitable tone ('Let us work together to…'). You keep up a consistent view, with some evidence to support your attitude to school dress or charities. Some suitable features of style help opinions ('I wonder how much we can raise…').	1, 2, 3	
You keep the reader's attention by the consistent tone, e.g. direct and lively. You give a clear point of view e.g. by trying to put events in perspective ('It is only for one day of term…') Suitable features of style add interest, e.g. sharing a joke ('Do you think Mr Jones would look good in a baseball cap?...')	4, 5, 6	
You keep the reader's interest by varying approach, e.g. moving from discussing money-raising to reasons for dressing suitably. You develop a clear point of view e.g. by distinguishing between personal and others' views ('Some people wouldn't bother…but I think that…'). You use different features of style to invite a response, e.g. to sum up, to ask questions ('What are we going to do about it?')	7, 8, 9	
You fulfil the purpose of the task by provoking a response in the listener, e.g. by making the listener want to join in. The viewpoint you have adopted allows different views towards school dress to be explored. Individual style is used to convey a particular viewpoint e.g. humour, sarcasm ('I can just see all the teachers wearing their Nike football shirts!').	10	

Sentence structure, punctuation and text organisation	Mark awarded	Your mark
You use simple connectives (*and, but, so*) to link parts of sentences. You write mostly in the first person ('I') and you use the present tense to give some opinions about dressing-up. You use simple adjectives to give a little bit of detail ('best clothes', 'smart looks') You use capital letters and full stops in places.	0	
Your sentences are mostly correct with a little variety e.g. connectives to explain ideas ('When we wear school uniform...') or different subjects of sentences to make things clearer ('Our fashion sense is shown.....We like to be seen...'). Different verb types are used to help explain ('When you are choosing your own clothes, I think that...') Each section or paragraph is about a different aspect of the day. You use capital letters and full stops correctly, with some other punctuation.	1, 2	
You use some different sentence types help to give opinions on the topic ('If we care about the charity we are supporting, we should...') Extra adjectives give detail and attitudes ('an exciting, worthwhile occasion'). The main ideas in each section are supported by reasons. Nearly all sentences are correctly punctuated, with some punctuation within sentences.	3, 4	
You use different sentence lengths and types to add variety, e.g. subordinate clauses to support opinions ('Although school uniform is practical it can also be boring...') You start sentences differently to emphasise points ('Unless you want to let the side down, you...'). Ideas are linked within paragraphs by the use of such things as lists leading to a climax ('The more we raise...then we can...eventually...'), connecting phrases ('As last time...'), and contrasts ('On the one hand...but you might say...'). Punctuation is used reliably and clearly to mark the structure of the sentences.	5	
A good range of sentence types makes interesting reading. A variety of sentence types, lengths and verb forms develops the opinions and comments. Instructions are clear, logical and rousing because of the arrangement of ideas within sections. A range of punctuation is used to make meaning clear and add to effects.	6	

Spelling	Mark awarded	Your mark
You have kept your words simple so that you can spell most of them, but you need to take care with words that sound the same, e.g. *there/their*; *were/ where*; *practice/practise*.	1	
You have tried to use bigger words, and have spelt the simple and common words correctly, but still need to be careful with words which sound the same, e.g. *weather/whether*; *affect/effect*.	2	
You can spell complex common and regular words correctly, but you may have problems with endings, e.g. *reducible/reducable*; *fulfil/fulfill*; *dependent/ dependant*. Combinations of vowels may also give you trouble, e.g. *receive/ recieve*; *brief/breif*; *weird/wierd*.	3	
You have tried to think of a wide range of vocabulary, so that you have used irregular and complicated words as well as common ones, and you have spelt most of them right. Your spelling is almost perfect apart from the occasional error.	4	

Total marks possible for Paper 3 Section A:

TWELFTH NIGHT
Section B

order to work out what level you would be awarded for the answer you have written, do the
lowing:

Read the assessment guidance given **for each level.** (ie **Level 4**)

Then read carefully the **Typical remarks** section. This provides examples of the sorts of
comments and points that will have been made by a student working at this level. Of
course, you will not have written exactly the same remarks, but you should be able to tell
if the **quality** of your writing is similar.

Now see if you can match *your* answer to a level. If you are unsure, ask someone you can
trust – a relative or a friend – to help you.

Once you have decided what level your answer would probably be given, look at the column
headed '**How to improve your level**'. This suggests what you need to do to improve your
answer so that you can do better next time, and achieve a higher level.

How well did you do?

Level 4   *3-6 marks*

In a level 4 answer there will be an
attempt to write in the first person, as
Feste, with a little explanation of what
happened when Malvolio caught the
drunks in the cellar and how Feste
teased Malvolio later when he dressed
up as the priest, Sir Topas. There may
be the odd quotation used.

Typical remarks in a level 4 answer:

was with Sir Toby and Sir Andrew in the cellar
f Olivia's house. We were having a good time
nd Maria fetched us plenty of wine and beer.
Ve were singing and dancing when Malvolio
ame in and told us to be quiet or he would tell

Olivia, but we just laughed at him. Then Maria
thought of a plan to write a letter pretending to
be Olivia, 'I can write very like my lady,' to make
Malvolio look a fool. We all thought it was
hilarious. After the trick had worked a treat, Sir
Toby told me to dress up and treat Malvolio like a
madman. Malvolio was very upset.

How to improve your level

1 Try to explain how Feste sees Malvolio
   and the other characters.

2 Use more quotations from the scenes
   to support what Feste says.

3 Give Feste's opinions on what was
   happening in these scenes and try to
   comment on both extracts equally.

How well did you do?

Level 5   *7-10 marks*

A level 5 answer will will show general understanding of how Feste sees the different situations and will explain his part in what happens. There will be quotations to support his remarks and opinions and both scenes will be covered equally.

Typical remarks in a level 5 answer:

What an old misery Mavolio is! I could not believe how he was so high-handed with Sir Toby, who is, after all, Olivia's uncle and a knight. But it was so funny when Sir Toby said, 'Sneck up!' I would like to tell him to shut up myself. But Maria thought of such a good plan to get back at him. She wrote a letter in Olivia's handwriting, giving Malvolio all sorts of ridiculous instructions. It all worked so well that Olivia let her uncle deal with the enemy and when Sir Toby had locked him up, I dressed up as a priest, Sir Topas. I pretended he was as mad as a hatter and I watched him get more and more upset.

How to improve your level

1 Give more details of the way in which the other characters argued with Malvolio in the first extract and how Feste twisted Malvolio's words in the second extract.

2 The characters in these scenes have some very funny lines which would appeal to Feste's sense of humour. Try to explore more of them.

3 The more of Feste's opinions you give, the more realistic your portrayal of his character will be.

How well did you do?

Level 6   *11–14 marks*

In a level 6 answer, the role of Feste will be convincing, showing clear understanding of the jokes he makes and his enjoyment of playing tricks. There will be enough detail about each scene to show the reader how the plot has moved on.

Typical remarks in a level 6 answer:

Things have certainly livened up in this house since Sir Toby came to stay. Lady Olivia has taken the deaths of her relatives far too hard but at least Sir Toby realises that life must go on. It was an excellent drinking session the other night, (with the other two knights!) until old Malvolio came in, pretending he was only carrying out Olivia's orders, 'My lady bade me tell you, that, though she harbours you as her kinsman, she's nothing allied to your disorders'. He went on to say that she might have to bid Sir Toby farewell, so Sir Toby and I began singing, 'Farewell, dear heart, since I must needs be gone'; Malvolio was not amused.

It was even funnier when Sir Toby asked him, 'Dost thou think , because thou art virtuous, there shall be no more cakes and ale?' Everyone joined in against Malvolio and he left. I had to use my acting skills later on when Maria's trick on Malvolio had worked and he was locked up for a lunatic. When he mentioned his lady, I pretended to be scandalised that he should be thinking of women all the time. After all, I was supposed to be Sir Topas, the priest. I also pretended that he was in a light room with large windows, not a poky, dark dungeon, which was the reality.

How to improve your level

1 Explain that Malvolio was a puritan, that they were had a very high profile in Shakespearean society, and that Shakespeare was making fun of them here.

2 Feste was a professional comedian, but in these scenes was working a little beyond his job description. Try to incorporate this idea.

3 You might try to copy some of Feste's speech patterns to make your portrayal of him even more convincing.

Level 7   *15-18 marks*

There will be a clear focus here, not only on Feste's character and his role in these scenes, but also on the plot development and the relationships between the other characters. There will be an understanding of the effects of language and some of the social mores of the time. Feste will be convincing.

Typical remarks in a level 7 answer:

Marry, what a trick it has been! When Maria first suggested her 'device', we knew it would bring Malvolio down to size and also give us some entertainment, but I did not realise it would last so long, and I wonder if it has gone a little too far. It is all very well for Sir Toby and his stupid fop, Sir Andrew, to make fun of a steward, but I am a paid fool and need to keep in favour with my employers. However, I can't help laughing when I think of how that pompous ass came down to the cellar to spout his puritanical propaganda. We all took exception to it and were voluble in our rudeness. The ensuing fiasco of the letter trick was equally hilarious, and Olivia's putting Malvolio into Sir Toby's custody was better than we could have hoped. It allowed us to lock up Malvolio as a lunatic, though we know he is not really insane, and we then had more entertainment when I visited him in the role of Sir Topas, contradicting everything he said and pretending to be scandalised at his words. I am not now sure, however, how I can get out of the situation without getting into trouble with my employers. The truth must come out in the end.

Where to find more help

Collins Total Revision KS3 English contains several chapters on how to answer questions on Shakespeare plays effectively.

HENRY V
Section A

he Test markers will assess your writing under the headings of:

'Composition and effect'

id

'Sentence structure, punctuation and text organisation'.

omposition and effect' means the overall effect of your writing – the views you express, and e variety and stylistic features you use to get those views across to the reader, in this case, e Test marker.

entence structure, punctuation and text organisation' means exactly what it says, and refers the way you express yourself in terms of the sentences you use (for example, is what you say ade clear by your choice of sentence structure?), the punctuation you select to organize those ntences – and the order and sequence of ideas *within* sentences and paragraphs.

here is also a further set of marks for spelling.

> assess your own writing, use the tables on the pages that follow and put in the final column e marks for your article which you think best fit the description given.

Composition and effect	Mark awarded	Your mark
You write that you were angry and, in simple terms, what caused your anger. You are also aware of the reader of the letter and write in an appropriate style.	0	
You try to make your writing interesting and you give a clear account of what was the situation or the incident that made you angry and what you did as a result. You take rather more care in choosing your words and are aware of the reader of the letter.	1, 2, 3	
You try to think of as many different words as possible for each thought about the situation or the incident you describe. You choose an informal and direct style for the friend you are writing to, and you express your anger forcefully. You also mention the result of your anger and what you did about it. Your letter clearly has a purpose.	4, 5, 6	
As you make your words as exact as possible, you are aware of how they will affect your friend who is reading the letter. You organise your writing carefully to make it interesting, and give plenty of detail about the situation or incident that made you angry and what you did about it. Your style is direct and informal, and you make the tone convincing.	7, 8, 9	
You use a wide range of words in order to interest your friend and persuade him/her of the just reasons for your anger. You do this by a full, detailed explanation of the situation or incident that made you angry. You distinguish clearly between this cause and what you did about it subsequently. The form of your letter is well controlled, the purpose is clear and the style is convincing.	10	

Sentence structure, punctuation and text organisation	Mark awarded	Your mark
You mark the pauses in your writing by using commas and occasionally full stops. Your sentences are simply constructed, but describe the situation or the incident clearly.	0	
Your use of full stops is mostly accurate. Some paragraphing is used, and you can expand longer sentences by using connectives such as *when, and, but, then.* There is some variation in sentence length and structure in order to develop points.	1, 2	
Paragraphs and an introduction give some form to the letter, developing your main ideas. There is some range of sentence structures. There is some variation in verb forms, which are well controlled (e.g. *I was angry at the time, but now I realise that this kind of thing will always exist*). Commas, full stops, capital letters and question marks are used correctly.	3, 4	
You give the relevant information clearly at the beginning and then use a new paragraph for each new development of the situation or incident, or reflections on your feelings and behaviour. You convey clear meaning by your accurate use of full stops, capital letters, commas, question marks, inverted commas and apostrophes. You vary the lengths of the sentences to produce different effects, and you make all subjects and verbs agree. You are well aware of the letter form.	5	
The paragraphs develop your ideas in order, and the situation or the incident are described with great clarity. The final paragraph draws conclusions about your reactions and feelings and what the experience has taught you. You use a variety of verb forms, and the tense changes are well controlled (e.g. *I had been very angry but as I calmed down I could begin to see that it might have been for the best*). You use all the punctuation marks listed in the band above so that the organisation of the letter form is clear. You control the length and structure of your sentences in order to vary the pace of the writing.	6	

Spelling	Mark awarded	Your mark
You have kept your words simple so that you can spell most of them, but you need to take care with words that sound the same, e.g. *there/their*; *were/where*; *practice/practise*.	1	
You have tried to use bigger words, and have spelt the simple and common words correctly, but still need to be careful with words which sound the same, e.g. *weather/whether*; *affect/effect*.	2	
You can spell complex common and regular words correctly, but you may have problems with endings, e.g. *reducible/reducable*; *fulfil/fulfill*; *dependent/dependant*. Combinations of vowels may also give you trouble, e.g. *receive/recieve*; *brief/breif*; *weird/wierd*.	3	
You have tried to think of a wide range of vocabulary, so that you have used irregular and complicated words as well as common ones, and you have spelt most of them right. Your spelling is almost perfect apart from the occasional error.	4	

Total marks possible for Paper 3 Section A: 2

HENRY V
Section B

order to work out what level you would be awarded for the answer you have written, do the
llowing:

- Read the assessment guidance given **for each level.** (ie **Level 4**)

- Then read carefully the **Typical remarks** section. This provides examples of the sorts of
  comments and points that will have been made by a student working at this level. Of
  course, you will not have written exactly the same remarks, but you should be able to tell
  if the **quality** of your writing is similar.

- Now see if you can match *your* answer to a level. If you are unsure, ask someone you can
  trust – a relative or a friend – to help you.

- Once you have decided what level your answer would probably be given, look at the column
  headed '**How to improve your level'.** This suggests what you need to do to improve your
  answer so that you can do better next time, and achieve a higher level.

How well did you do?

Level 4   *3-6 marks*

A level 4 answer will give a summary of
the contents of the speeches of Henry
and the other characters. It will select
parts of them without commenting on
the overall purpose and meaning. It will
describe the nature of Henry's anger,
and his urging of the soldiers into battle
with no mention of the cause which
motivates him. It may mention Henry's
anger or Montjoy's sadness without
describing the background of these. It is
this background which relates to the
reason for Henry's anger, and this is the
question.

Typical remarks in a level 4 answer:

Henry wants to really get his men going to attack
the town of Harfleur. Now that he has finally got to
France, he wants to push them on to succeed and
get the job done. Henry is also extremely mad when
he knows of the death of the boys and he wants to

fight some French horsemen who are on the hill in
front of them. On the field, Henry has slaughtered
common men, princes and mercenary soldiers.

How to improve your level

1 You should deal with the whole
   speeches of Henry and Montjoy, and
   not just pick out parts of them.

2 The question asks you to show how the
   rightness of his cause makes Henry's
   anger so fierce, and any details from
   the speeches that you want to use
   should be related to this. State this
   near the beginning of your answer, and
   keep referring back to it as you make
   each point.

3 Explain how your points are relevant
   to the text and the question, and
   support this by giving quotations from
   the speeches. When you write
   quotations, write them out in lines of
   poetry as they are in the text.

How well did you do?

Level 5   *7–10 marks*

A level 5 answer will provide much more detail from the text, including quotations which will be written out properly. The purpose of the speeches may be mentioned at the start, but the continuing relevance may not be clear. The answer will seem to be full because it will usually follow the meaning of the speeches point by point. There may also be descriptive comments about Henry's character and some reference to the general action of the play.

Typical remarks in a level 5 answer:

Henry is convinced of the justice of his cause because the leaders of the Church in England told him so. Because of this, he is determined to win this battle, and defeat the citizens of Harfleur and take the town. This is the first part of his conquest of France:

> 'On, on, you noble English,
> Whose blood is fet from fathers of
>   war-proof! – '

In the second extract, we see Henry in the heat of battle, very angry at the thought that French soldiers escaping from the battle have needlessly killed the boys left in the tents:

> 'I was not angry since I came to France
> Until this instant.'

This stirs Henry to action, and he threatens what he will do to his prisoners and how he will fight some French soldiers nearby:

> '…we'll cut the throats of those we have
> And not a man of them that we shall take
> Shall taste our mercy'.

This shows that Henry, in his anger, can be a man of strong and cruel action when he needs to be. The French herald, Montjoy, shows by what he says how the action in the battle was devastating.

How to improve your level

1 There is an adequate number of quotations now, and they are written out properly, but they might be built into the sentence rather better rather than just added on.

2 Analyse the way Henry speaks and acts, and point out what it tells us about his character, because the reason for his anger and the justice of his cause is what the question is concerned with.

3 Show how Henry relates to those around him, and describe the effect on them of his words and actions – for instance, how he must inspire the army, and how he must have terrified the French soldiers in the battle of Agincourt. Give plenty of detail from the text.

Level 6 *11–14 marks*

A level 6 answer will consist of a full and detailed account of both speeches, but all points made will be relevant to the question of the motive for Henry's ferocity. He feels that it is his duty as their King and commander to rouse his men to warlike action. All references and quotations will be similarly relevant. It is also Henry's outraged feelings for the boys and the cowardly murders that have occurred, that stir him to ferocious anger in the second extract.

Typical remarks in a level 6 answer:

When Henry is urging his army to attack Harfleur without mercy or any deviation from his purpose, and his speech is strong and aggressive. He is full of confidence, energy and determination, and shouts that they will win victory, whatever the cost:

'Once more unto the breach, dear friends, once
    more;
Or close the wall up with our English dead!
In peace there's nothing so becomes a man
As modest stillness and humility:
But when the blast of war blows in our ears,
Then imitate the action of the tiger;
Stiffen the sinews, summon up the blood,
Disguise fair nature with hard-favour'd rage.'

In the second extract, Montjoy describes the hideous bloodshed at Agincourt, but only after we see that Henry is stirred to action by his feelings for the boys who have been killed:

'I was not angry since I came to France
Until this instant.'

The overwhelming strength of the menace at the beginning of this speech shows how angry Henry is, and Montjoy's account of what he is looking for on the field of battle shows what Henry is capable of when he is roused.

How to improve your level

1 Give a sensitive response to the power and force of Henry's speech before Harfleur. Comment on the language.

2 Quote the most powerful images in the speech and make them relevant to Henry's conviction that his cause is right. Comment on the feelings that motivate Henry in the second extract and compare them with his ferocious behaviour at Agincourt.

3 Show how he is, above all, always in perfect control of his feelings, and trace their strength and pace, how they rise and then settle down.

How well did you do?

Level 7   *15-18 marks*

A level 7 answer will show that each part of each extract is related to the question of Henry's anger and conviction that he is right. The answer will show a spirited response to the power and graphic imagery in Henry's speeches, and in that of Montjoy. The quality of the language will be explicitly commented upon and illustrated with relevant quotations. The strength of Henry's character will be pointed out and also emphasised as will be his perfect control of his feelings and of the situation in general. There will be reference to the submissive attitude of Montjoy.

Typical remarks in a level 7 answer:

Throughout the play, Henry's motivation has been that God is on his side and his cause is right. This is why, when he has to implement his will and his force, he is so strong, fearless and unhesitating. The ferocity and driving energy of his pre-battle speech to his soldiers must have inspired them and stirred them to action as nothing else could have done. Not only does he refer to tigers, sinews, blood, cannon, rocks, the 'wild and wasteful ocean' and one of the greatest warriors in history, Alexander the Great, but also to their

families back at home and their sense of patriotism, and says that it is for the honour of a these that they must succeed. There can surely be no better expression of pent-up aggression wanting to be released than this:

> 'For there is none of you so mean and base
> That hath not noble lustre in your eyes.
> I see you stand like greyhounds in the slips,
> Straining upon the start.'

At the blood-curdling conclusion of the speech, he mentions God, himself and St. George in the same breath, and we can assume he would have led the charge himself on horseback at the rousing climax of his speech:

> 'The game's afoot.
> Follow your spirit, and upon this charge
> Cry ' God for Harry, England and Saint
>   George!'

This total control of language reflects Henry's perfect control over his own actions and his soldiers. His anger rises again in the second extract, this time provoked, quite rightly, by the unspeakable horror of the murder of the defenceless boys. Seeing some French soldiers on a nearby hill, he sends his herald to tell them to come down, and says how…

> '…. we'll cut the throats of those we have;
> And not a man of them that we shall take
> Shall taste our mercy:– go, and tell them so.'

But he is still in total control because his cause is just on this occasion and throughout the play.

Where to find more help

Collins Total Revision KS3 English contains several chapters on how to answer questions on Shakespeare plays effectively.